STREAM

RABBIT HOUSE PRESS

Versailles, KY 40383

Published in the United States by Rabbit House Press August 2020.

For inquiries about author appearances and orders, please visit www.rabbithousepress.com.

Cover art: Indie Mentors by John Lackey
Illustrations: Petersen Thomas
Editors: Taylor Riley, Mary Anne Long & Erin Chandler
Cover design & interior formatting: Brooke Lee

ISBN: 978-1-7351727-2-9

STREAM

Kay Long Roberts

Contents

Dedication

Shelby Trails Park

A portion of funds received from the sale of this book will be donated to Shelby Trails Park.

In 2010, Dr. Roger and Diane Shott of Anchorage Kentucky gifted their beloved three hundred and eighty-seven acres to Shelbyville/Shelby County Parks and Recreation. They envisioned the land gift as a place where people of all ages can ride their own horse, rent a guided horseback ride, or learn to ride. Some might choose to hike, run trails, watch birds, or engage in other nature lovers' activities.

Ernie and Betty Middleton worked hand in hand with Roger and Diane to help design and shape the land. Ernie is now deceased, but the effects of his passion for nature lingers.

Clay Cottongim, Parks Director at the time of the gifting, helped develop and manage the land in accordance with the Shott's vision. He continues as a Park Consultant and invested volunteer. At this writing, Clay is overseeing the development of a Butterfly Field in honor of Ernie Middleton.

Shelby Trails Park has grown to include twenty-one horseback riding trails, a beautiful, thirty-two stall barn, and an indoor and outdoor arena for year-round riding. More improvements are planned.

For more information about Shelby Trails Park:

http://shelbycountyparks.com/our-parks/shelby-trails-park/

Acknowledgments

My grandfather Royce Thompson retired as a businessman and purchased nearly five hundred Western Kentucky rural acres. At age six, I began walking with him over this spacious grain and cattle farm. His gentle ambience and palpable love for the land settled in me.

The spaciousness of the land delighted me. But it was the beckoning complexity of the area preserved as raw nature that held my greatest attention—always.

My sister, Mary Anne Long, a retired English teacher, was a relentless encourager.

John C. Wright, MD, my life partner, and his daughters Tami Storm and Kim Murphy, were my first, go-to critique gurus.

Petersen Thomas, a Louisville artist and former textbook illustrator, approached the creation of his sketches with a renewed memory of his fondness for his special childhood stream.

Matthew Walsh was extremely helpful during the beginning stages of the book and I appreciate his artistry and contribution.

Taylor Riley, Editor, is an honored graduate of Spalding University MFA in Fine Arts in Creative Writing program and current editor of a local rural newspaper.

I appreciate the holistic influence of leaders, faculty, staff and student colleagues associated with Spalding University's MFA in Fine Writing program. I value our continuing relationship.

I acknowledge my precious sons, Joseph and Daniel Roberts, and their wives, Tami and Mary and grandchildren, Katie, Rachel, Hannah and Ariel.

Finally, without the gift of Shelby Trails Park by Dr. Roger and Diane Shott, there likely would be no walk, no horseback rides, no deer, no nested paths, no shadow pond, no butterfly fields, and no Stream. We, the travelers by horse and foot, offer gratitude.

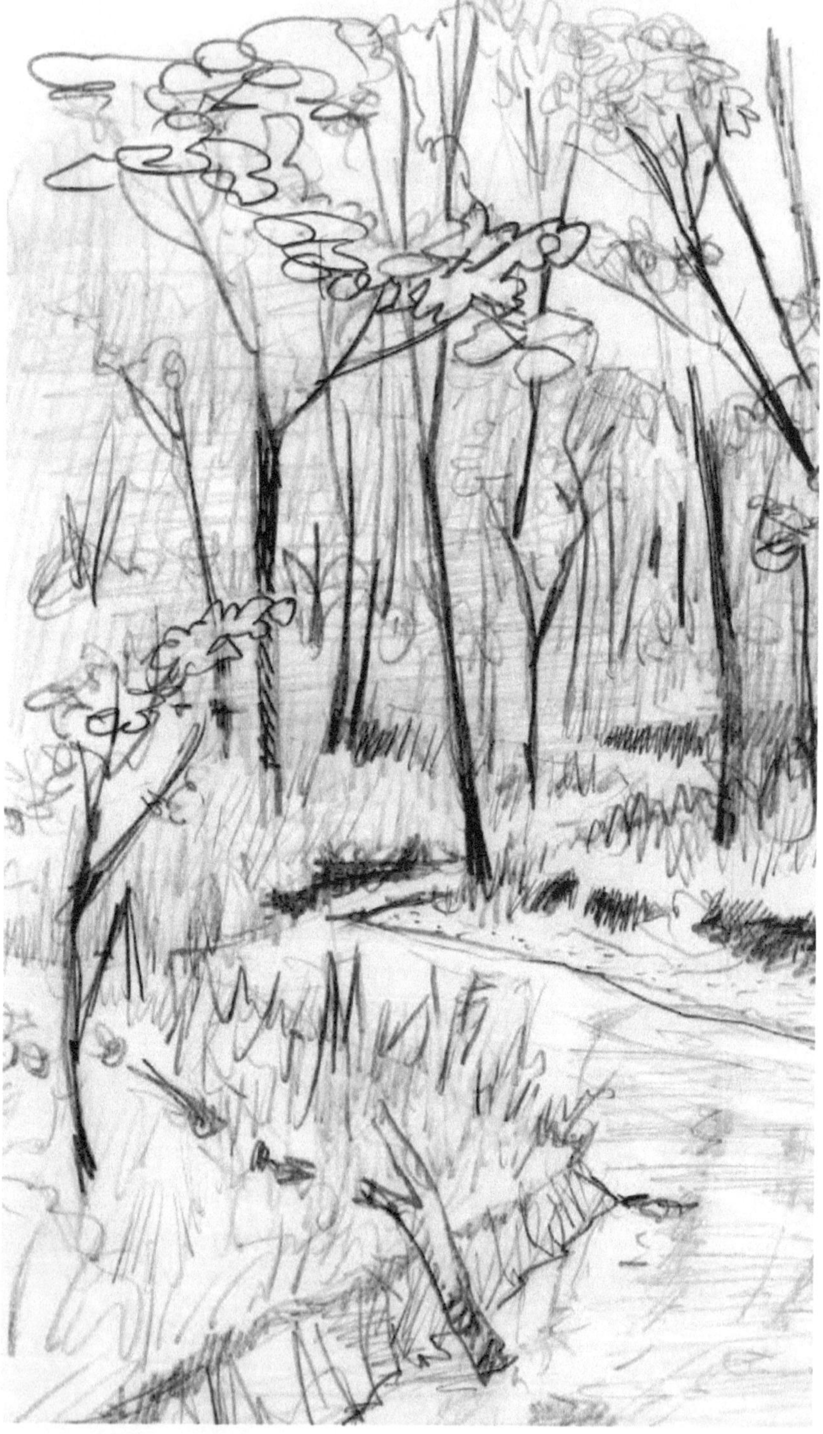

STREAM

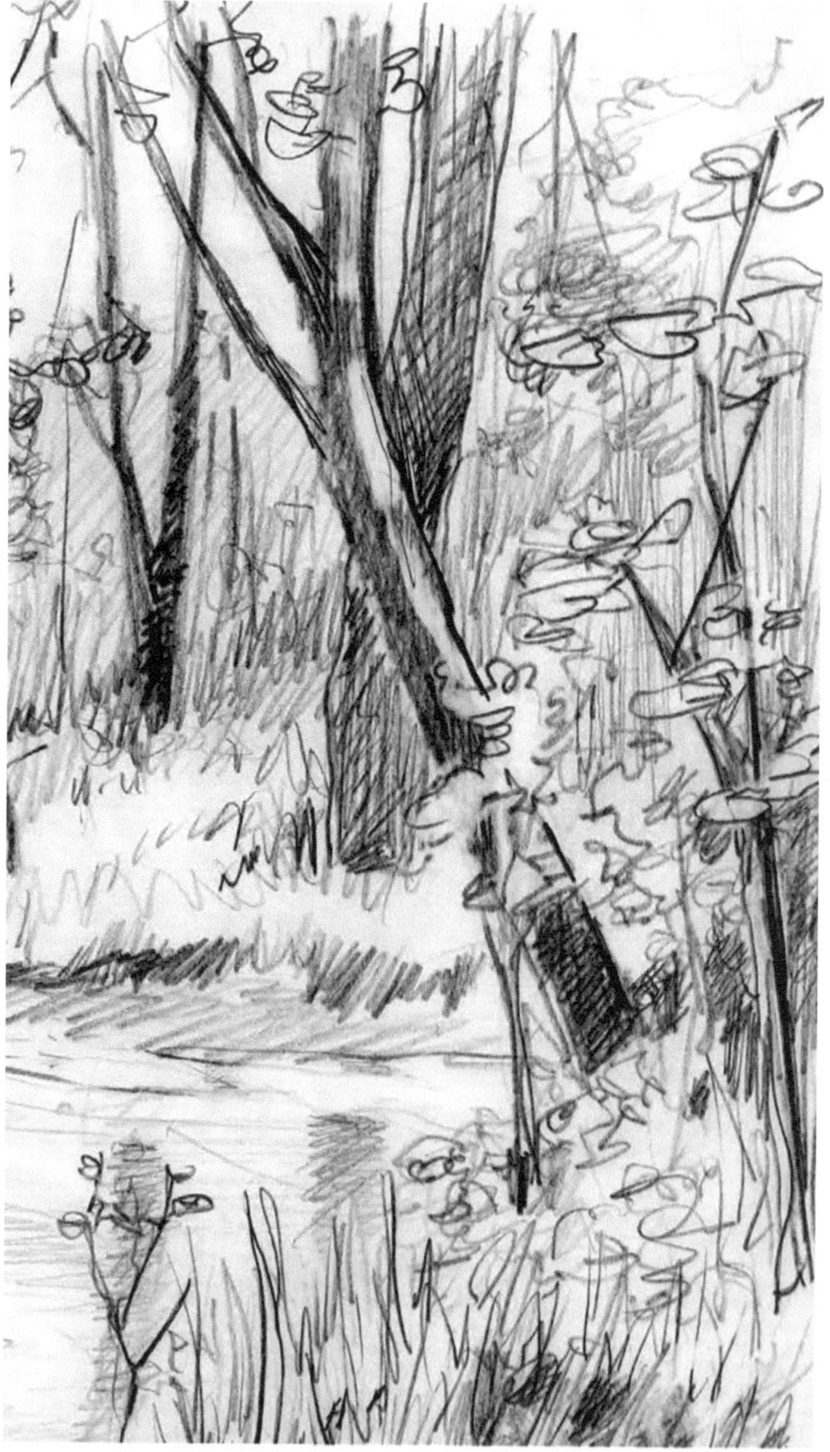

Waypoint One

Reverie

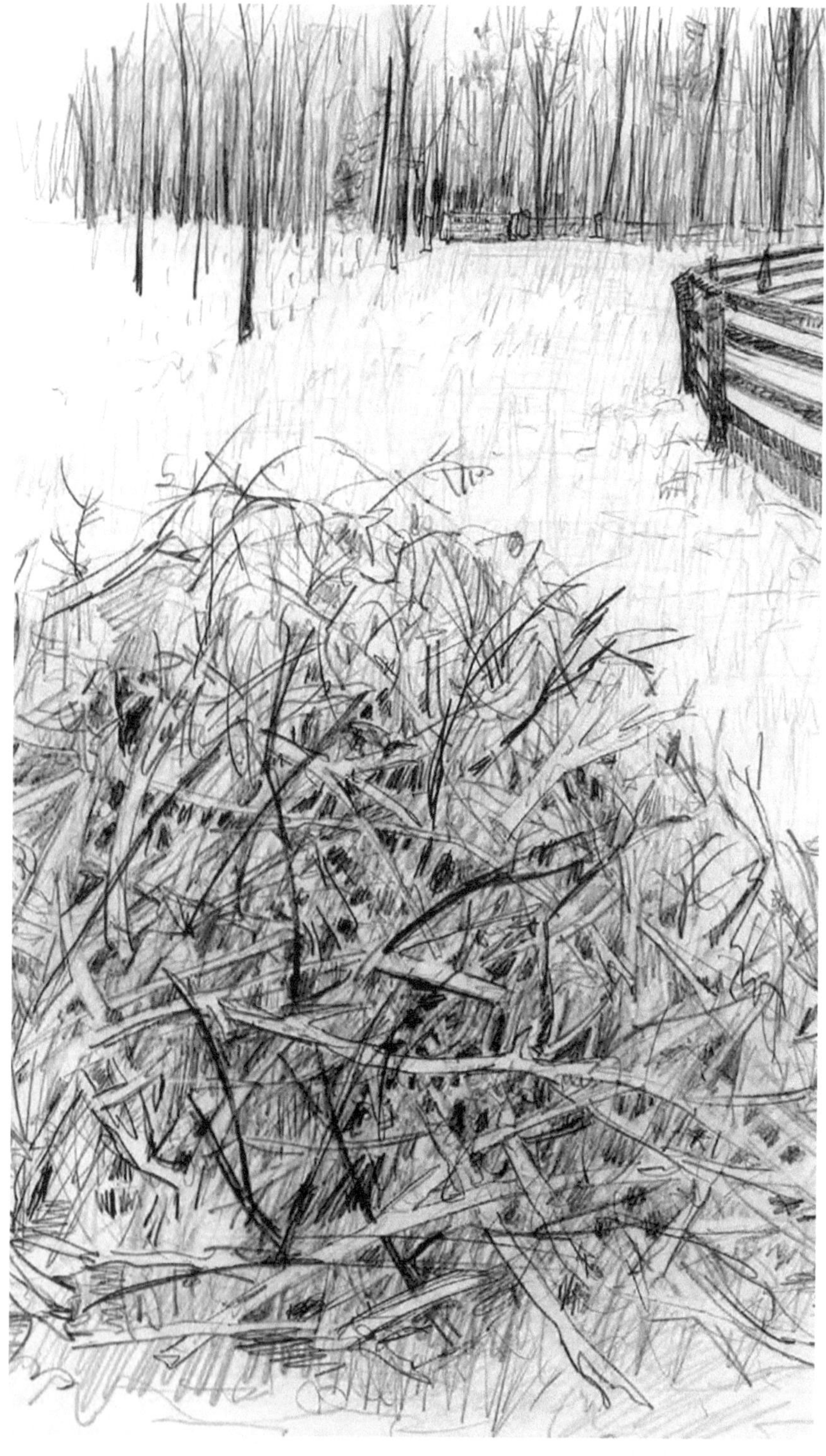

In the dawn of morning—just about every morning—after
feeding two Tennessee Walking horses,
I turn my lanky Caucasian X-chromosomes to the right of the
barn and amble down a familiar, sloping, stone covered path…
About sixty-five degrees grade.

I straighten my spine, push my chin and shoulders back, walk
forward, and thoughtfully step over several gullies, each uniquely
etched…
By powerful, determined rain.

Three-quarters down this hill, I pause just a few seconds and
absorb my first glimpse of Stream.

Beneath this path I stand upon, a mystic waterway flows north to
south from distant farms.

Stream enters on my left side and flows right through a buried,
large round steel throughway.

I stand firm for a moment to sense the tenor of flow and…
To scour for danger.

Sometimes Stream is dry, sometimes filled with rainwater, maybe
overflowing, maybe merely wet, or dangerous but…
Always meandering.

Today, various insects linger just above a quiet Stream, then
quickly flit from place to place.

When I am past, birds, mice, squirrels, rabbits, coyotes, and other
creatures recapture their place with Stream.

The sun sits at sixty percent of its journey upward, directly in
front of me…
As I walk Eastward.

Another quarter down this path, I reach the edge of a flat, three-acre field where two old mares will later graze.

Alongside will be their two, adult offspring: half-sister and half- brother, each sired by the same bold, black Stallion.

All four horses are now held captive from the surrounding abundance of nature by harsh, ugly wire…
I feel sad.

I notice the copious, multi-shaped mounds of dried horse manure; the faltering, scattered twenty-or-so trees, at least twelve marked by blight.

I recall a once opulent center grove with about fifteen lush trees standing as a circle, staying harsh sun, holding coolness inside.

I remember these same four horses, lingering peacefully within the circle, their tails swishing flies, moving shaded, cooler air…
Over their hot bodies.

Today I see trees with peeling bark of listless color and small and large branches scattered atop dry brown grass, even as green grass peeks up.

A familiar longing tightens my chest, as I helplessly watch these once strong, lofty trees yield…
To Emerald Ash Borers.

Straight ahead, the locked black steel gate opens a path out of this prison. But first, I must pass the voluminous pile of dead branches, merely waiting to be burned…
Without celebration, without marshmallows.

Just beyond this wood pile I see the empty, black-boarded horse ring. My mind recalls the two younger horses—yearlings then— pacing round the ring, paying scarce attention to my latest trial of a newly read, training technique.

The horses, now twenty-eight years, still ignore my commands…
I smile.

Some days, I recall watching Andrew, a five-pound midnight
black Maltipoo, jump in and out of the ring, fiercely barking as
horses canter round and round, the horses often shying sideways
to be careful not to step on him…
I see them nuzzle Andrew softly as they rest.

Outside this caged land, Nature's changing scenery wraps
three- hundred-sixty degrees around the field, always lush as I
see it. Never mind whether red, green, brown, orange, white,
or varied colors.

My mind settles there for a time and I remember other days and
years. I inhale deeply and lock the precious visions inside me…
Sometimes, I think I feel even what I cannot see.

To my right, at a mere distance beyond the wire fence, I see a
narrow horse trail alongside Stream's side. The trail is quiet this
morning, but I can see the riders in my mind. I remember when I
was with them.

On the far and near sides of this path, rows of nature's varied
trees—elm, oak, birch, cedar, pine, sycamore, others—coddle the
path…
As if to keep it hidden—safe.

Through spaces between the trees, I catch glimpses of Stream. A
rush of blood pulses in me. Stream is where life has happened, for
a very long time…
When I gaze at Stream, I feel the timelessness.

I step forward from the end of my downward path, onto the flat
field. I walk past the dying trees, past the pile of dead limbs, past
the empty training circle to a steel gate.

I open the steel latch, walk quickly through and turn left…
Onto free land.

Once outside the gate, I must choose to turn immediately left again and follow the wire fence back toward the horse barn—or to move forward straight ahead…
I always move forward.

Another fifteen easy steps, I come to a juncture—one path to the left, one straight ahead, another to the right—all paths nestled between dense foliage…
The right path leads to Stream.

As I step forward, I surprise two peacefully grazing doe and three fawns who also surprise me. One doe lifts her head, stiffens her body and snorts. The others quickly turn to look and almost simultaneously leap into the air, aimed rightward—flip their white tails toward me—and disappear into the woods. This happens so very often…
Still, I jump each time.

Four steps forward and finally, I reach the path to the right—the one I seek.

Bird calls, from many different species, become louder. They blend and confuse me as I try to sort them. I think I recognize the chirps of sparrows, fee-bee calls of phoebes, harsh caw-caw of crows, chur-chur of Northern Red Cardinals, guttural cooing of mourning doves, and farther by the hidden pond, the oo-eek of female wood ducks on frantic flight away from intruders.

But Nature exceeds my skills—still! I think that I should be certain, but I yield. I allow the sounds to mix, to mingle…
To merely be.

My breath softens. Sometimes, I feel joined with all I see, even the air. My friends who also walk or ride this way say…
They feel the same.

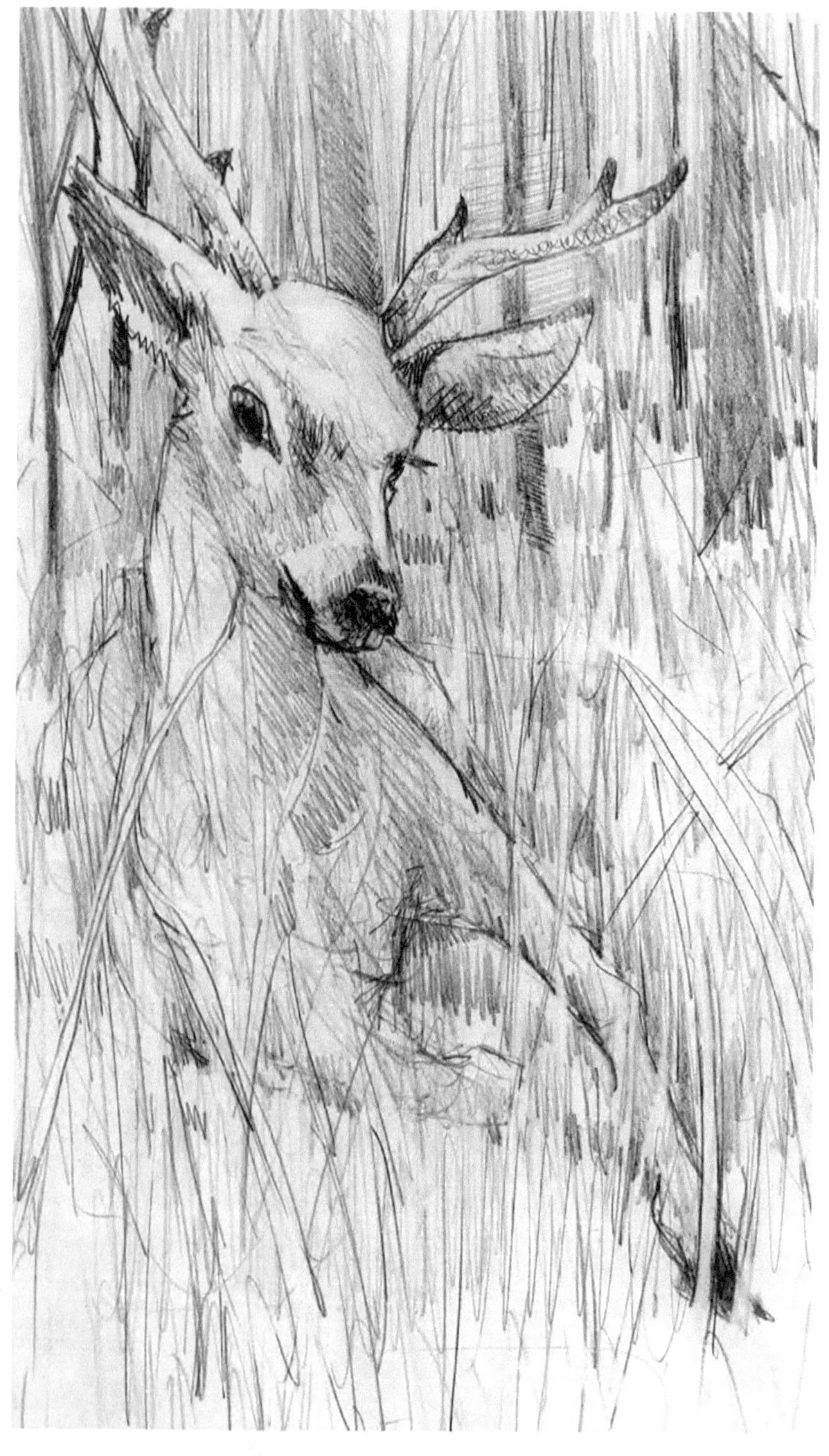

Waypoint Two

A Luckless Deer

I take the right turn and walk onto a nestled hallway that lies between dense trees. It is an uneven walk—fifty steps forward at a thirty-degree grade—then sixty-seven steps on flat surface to reach the adjoining field.

Stones of different shapes and size, uneven soil carved by steel horse shoes on wet days, and changing light as clouds pass over, make this path a tricky walk.

Hulls of broken nuts left by hungry squirrels, mice, and rats, crunch under my boots.

About midway on this path, I walk across yet a different section of Stream that flows under and across my path via a steel tunnel.

This stream is often dry but when wet, it carries water, mud, sticks, and critters southward, toward Stream. I think of it as a cousin, an offshoot of Stream.

This stream was birthed in higher land. It is weaker than Stream. But in high rain, this stream—and its Meandering cousins—will join with Stream at different junctures…

Together, they become a mighty force.

I move forward. My intended journey is straight ahead, across the adjoining field to Stream…

But not yet.

As I exit this path, out of the corner of my eye, on my left side, I see a glimpse of something out of place, something different. On the ground, between two rows of dense trees, I turn and see a crumpled mass lying…

So very still.

Around this object, I see Mayhem.

Many different birds of different sizes swoop down and land atop the lifeless object. They hop, flap, fly up and down, tweet, chirp, squawk, leave and return.

Despite this noise and busyness, the brown object does not move.

As I walk forward, the birds leave. A small mouse, maybe other creatures, scamper into the woods…
The air is quiet.

There, upon this warm land, is a small deer, a mere teenager lying very still. I move four steps closer and still he does not move. I see that he is dead.

His head is thrust backward, as if he had looked toward the sky and begged for life. His right front foot is turned under him…
As if he tried to push himself up.

The bullet of an unprepared, novice hunter who had no one to guide him was deadly—but not swift. The bullet merely wounded the young deer, so…
His painful death was slow.

Two, small, six-point antlers crown this youth's head. Had the deer lived, his antlers would have been majestic.

Here the Earth welcomes and absorbs him. He will slowly leave each day, as if melting. On perhaps the seventh day forward, I will walk by and not even see…
The fur that stays the longest time.

If not stolen, the antlers will remain for a time.

If not stolen, the antlers will feed rich calcium, phosphorous, and other minerals to his fellow field mice, squirrels, and foxes.

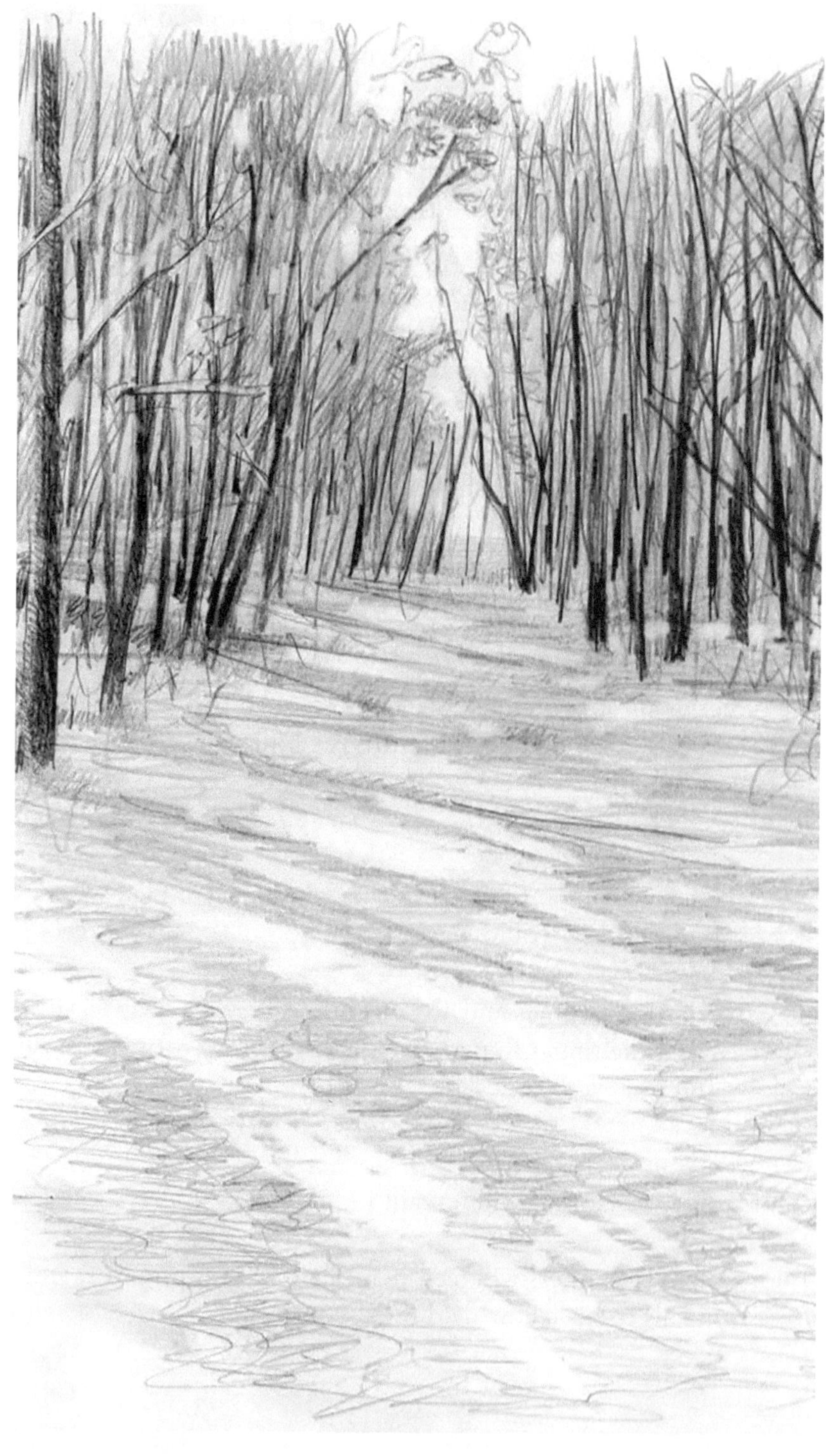

Waypoint Three

A Nested Path

The luckless deer diverted me from my eastward journey.
Without awareness, I continue walking north instead of east, still
pondering life and death. But then, I attend to spaces between the
not-yet-lush forest trees. I can see inside the spaces and I forget
big life dilemmas…

I only think of what I see and feel.

Then, I sense I am being watched and I glance sideways. There,
looking outward from the trees, I see a Doe and a Fawn,
deciding if they should flee. As I walk, I keep my body straight,
so I don't frighten them. A rabbit, a squirrel, a mouse, and a
wild, should-have-been-tamed cat…

Scurry across my path.

I pass a section of the land where one morning my ten-pound
Shih Tzu, Prince Charming, alias PC, walked with me. We turned
a corner and came upon a coyote feasting on a deer.

This small dog barked aggressively and bolted toward the coyote.
The startled coyote jumped and fled into the distant woods…
Still, PC pursued him.

Visions of other dogs torn to shreds by coyotes flashed in my
mind. I ran to stop him. Of course, I was too slow, but finally PC
returned, wagging his tail, happy with his attack…

The God of Nature protected this foolish dog.

I reach the pinnacle of this northward path. I must choose to go
straight forward or turn right, through an eastward path, about
eighty-seven steps, toward Stream…

I turn right through this Nested Path.

This passageway flows between two groves of trees. The smell is
musky, the air is…

Cool, but warming.

The morning sun rises slowly. At Apex, it releases rays of light shaped like an open, hand-held, Japanese fan. Narrow at Apex, the rays grow broader as they descend their piercing trajectory through the tall, straight trees, finally striking Earth as an orchestra of sharp arrows.

Thin and broad, clear and muted…
The lights reveal the shadows of the woods.

At the end of this eighty-seven-step passage, I turn right again—this time south toward…
Stream.

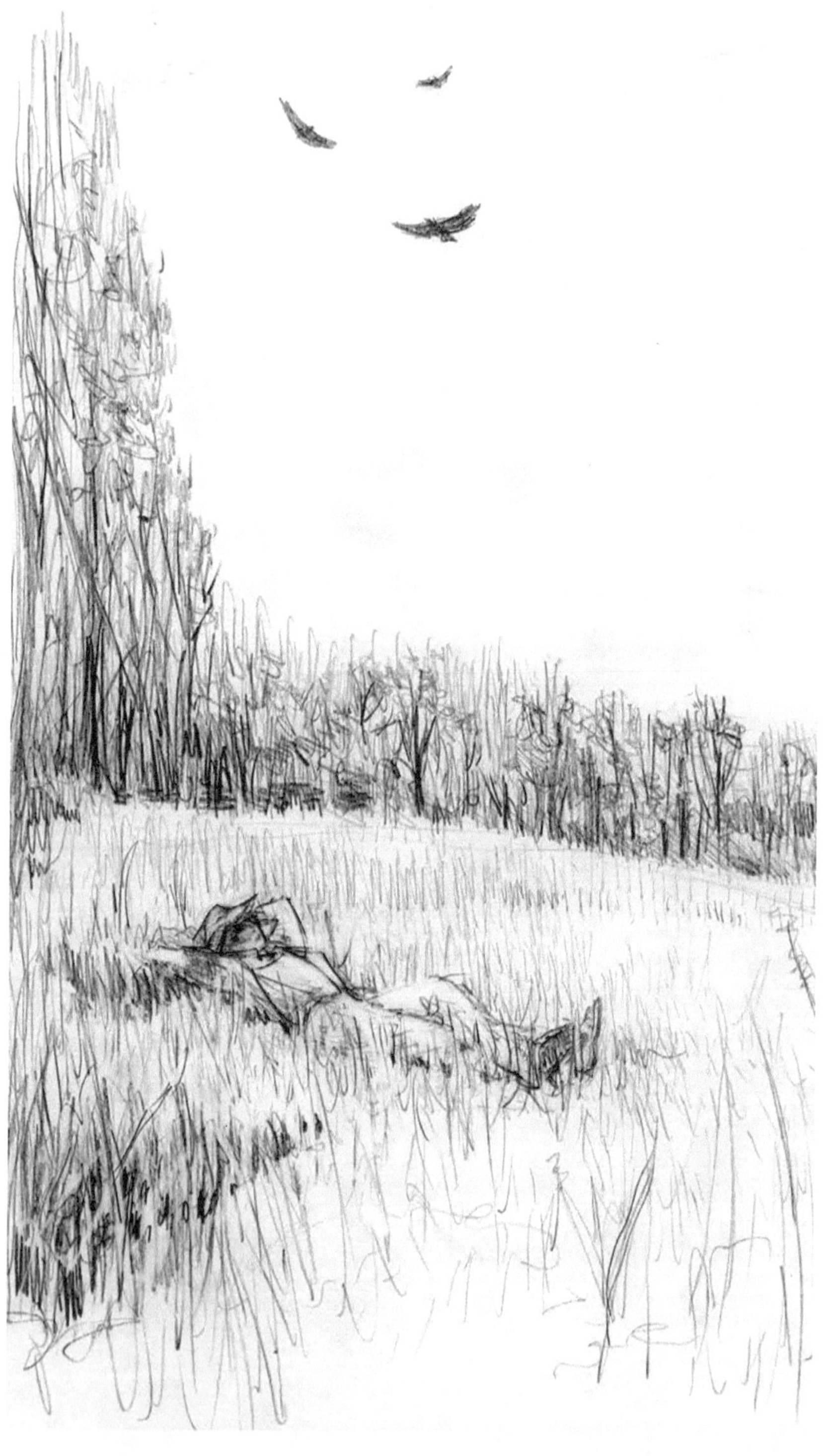

Waypoint Four

Sky Scan

A walk rarely lives only once. Memories recreate them.

Like today, when I stopped my journey for a minute or two to remember one past October day.

That morning was pleasantly cool, the air clean. I walked with no conscious thought.

When I stepped outside the shaded Nested Path, I felt the sun strike my shoulders, so…

I slowed my pace to let the warmth stay longer.

Another three steps forward and I layed upon the earth. Billed hat over my face, eyes closed, pleasant rays of sun falling on me…

I swear I felt the warmth reach inside me.

Not long into this reverie, I sensed shadows pass over me, a brief loss of sunlight. I opened my eyes and saw three large, dark, Turkey Vultures—still high in the sky, circling…

Soaring closer, closer, closer.

I had seen Turkey Vultures rip flesh apart with their long, sharp talons…

Effortlessly.

The Vultures' wings dipped smoothly left and right, like a plane eyeing a landing pad. Four other vultures flew toward them, to join the feast…

Me!

I quickly sat upright. Being breakfast was not what I had in mind. I waved my hands vigorously…

"I am not dead," I yelled.

In union, without exasperation, the Vultures smoothly changed their trajectory to a nearby wooded area…

Their feast was still missing.

My mind flashed to another warm day, when as a child, I walked
in another Woods with my Grandfather.

When he turned to me and said, "Nature will nourish you, Kay.
But be wary of surprises. And danger too!"

"For sure!" I muttered to myself.

19

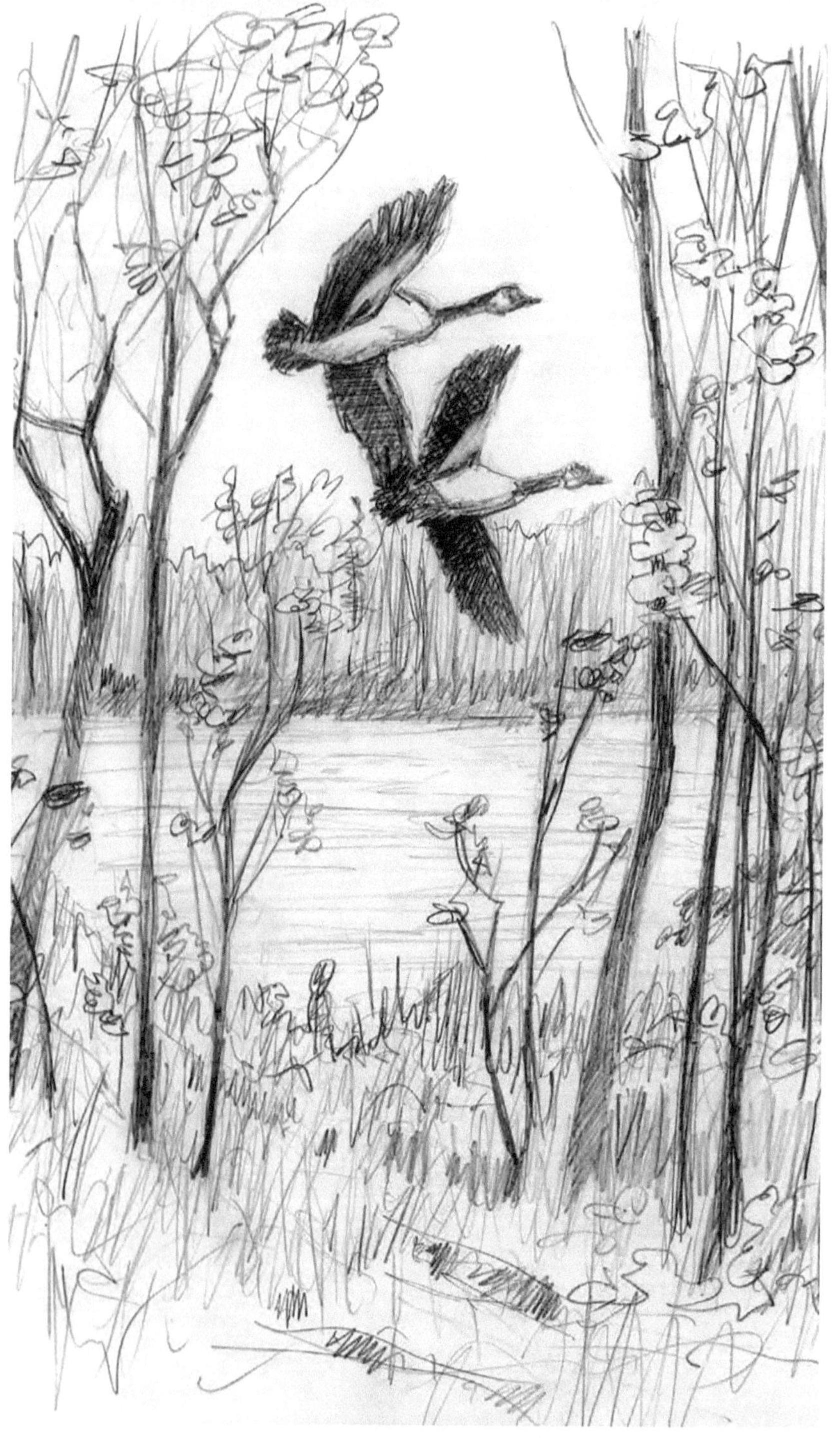

Waypoint Five

Shadow Pond

Oops!

I almost forgot to visit Shadow Pond—just a few steps straight
across from where I just turned right…

> *I always visit Shadow Pond!*

Shadow Pond is easily missed by a non-observant passerby.
Unruly dense trees, weeds, cattails, and other wild foliage
surround it. Sunlight casts shadows, but no bright reflections
that might catch one's eye. And, its surface is a mere distance
from its muddy bottom…

> *I have never seen the water clear.*

Sounds hearken the presence of Shadow Pond.

No matter how stealthily I approach—before I can see through
the brush—I hear the croak of a male frog, followed instantly by a
loud Splash.
Another second and the air fills with harsh honking, wings
flapping…

> *As geese soar over me.*

Shadow Pond is mostly round, yet a little bit too long and a
little bit too square to say so. At its upper right corner, water
overflows southward into yet another of Stream's meandering
streams, and…

> *Keeps the pond shallow.*

Delayed too long, I walk forward, toward Stream.

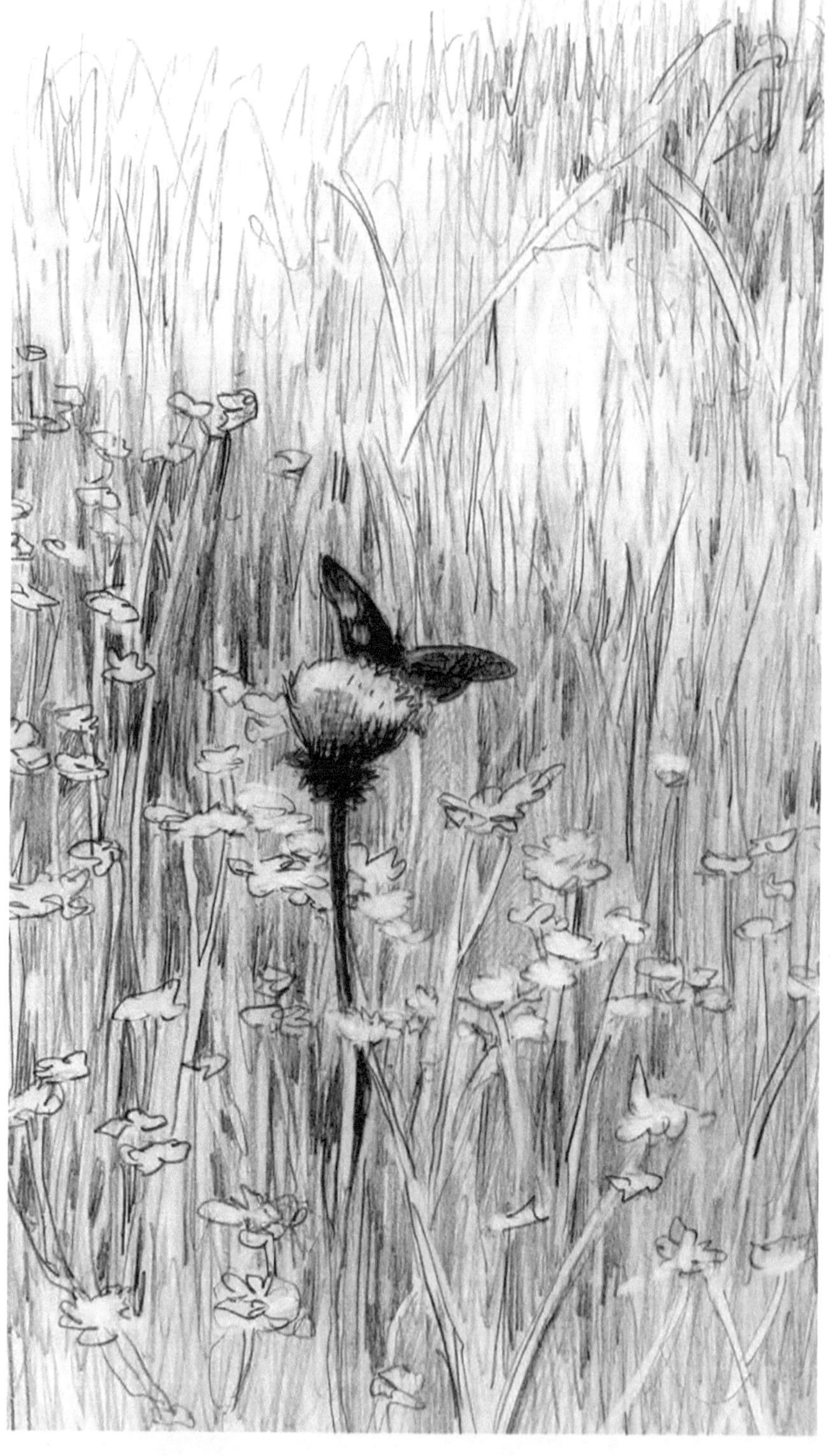

Waypoint Six

Butterfly Field

Still,

The time is early morning, the season is early Spring. I mosey southward.

Just a mere one-hundred-and-thirty good-sized steps farther to Stream.

Like the previous paths, this one is bounded by heavy brush. But, in between the brush, there is a greater space…

The size of a farmer's field. Maybe ten acres, about one-third cultivated…

Free is how I feel the space.

Today, this open field area is still brown. The grass is short with few weeds.

But I remember how the field will look, when the…

Season is fully Spring.

Thick, dark green grass will cover the cultivated portion, and multi-colored stems and blooms will reach up and out from the soil.

Bright rays of sun will strike the area nearest the brush and create a contrasting ambience that will appear muted, ethereal.

One who stills to look, will see a surreal, blurred yellow haze…

Just beyond the dark green grass.

Today, on the lower section of this land, where rainwater stands the longest—a few small stems already reach above the still short grass.

Usually, in April or May, this lower section will fill with a maze of stems of interesting designs, topped with artfully shaped weeds and flowers of many colors.

My mind already sees thirty or more multicolored butterflies, flitting here and there, stopping for mere seconds, seeking the most luscious nectar…

Often choosing a round, purple clover blossom perched upon a long stem.

I see the butterflies hover close to their chosen blossom; their wings beating perhaps fifty to eighty times per minute.

And when the space is just right, thrusting their long, thin, proboscis inside…

To quickly suck their gourmet meal.

The vision nudges me to remember a different jaunt, when I stood in the Louvre, in Paris, and looked upon Impressionist Art.

The paintings were muted, blended, mysterious, inviting and captivating.

I flew over an ocean to see these.

Yet, all the while…

That beauty was already here.

Deer often linger in this field to reap the harvest.

Today, just beyond the farthest edge of the field—where the brush begins,

I notice the tall, bark stripped tree that hosts a rotting deer stand, with

Weakened wooden steps that climb upward but hang crooked.

It is a Place where hunters wait to kill unsuspecting deer that stop to eat the grains of corn scattered on the ground.

I know the necessity to limit the deer population—to protect
nature—to ultimately protect deer themselves.

Unchecked there will be no forest, no habitat, no wildlife.
Still, I walk on, saddened.

Finally!

I am at the junction I seek. I turn and face left.

I can see Stream at the place we regularly meet. Just about
forty-five steps, fairly-straight-down a sixty-degree grade path...
Not a smooth path.

It is shaped by two deep gullies carved by rain, forbidden tires,
and occasional deep round tracks left by horses—and deer that
traveled when the soil was wet.
 Often, dead and green limbs droop from overhanging trees.

Just last year, a one-pound Horse Apple dropped, from one of
the several Osage Orange trees that line this path, directly on my
unsuspecting head!
I am careful now. I watch before I step.

Yeah!
I step onto this favorite path toward Stream.

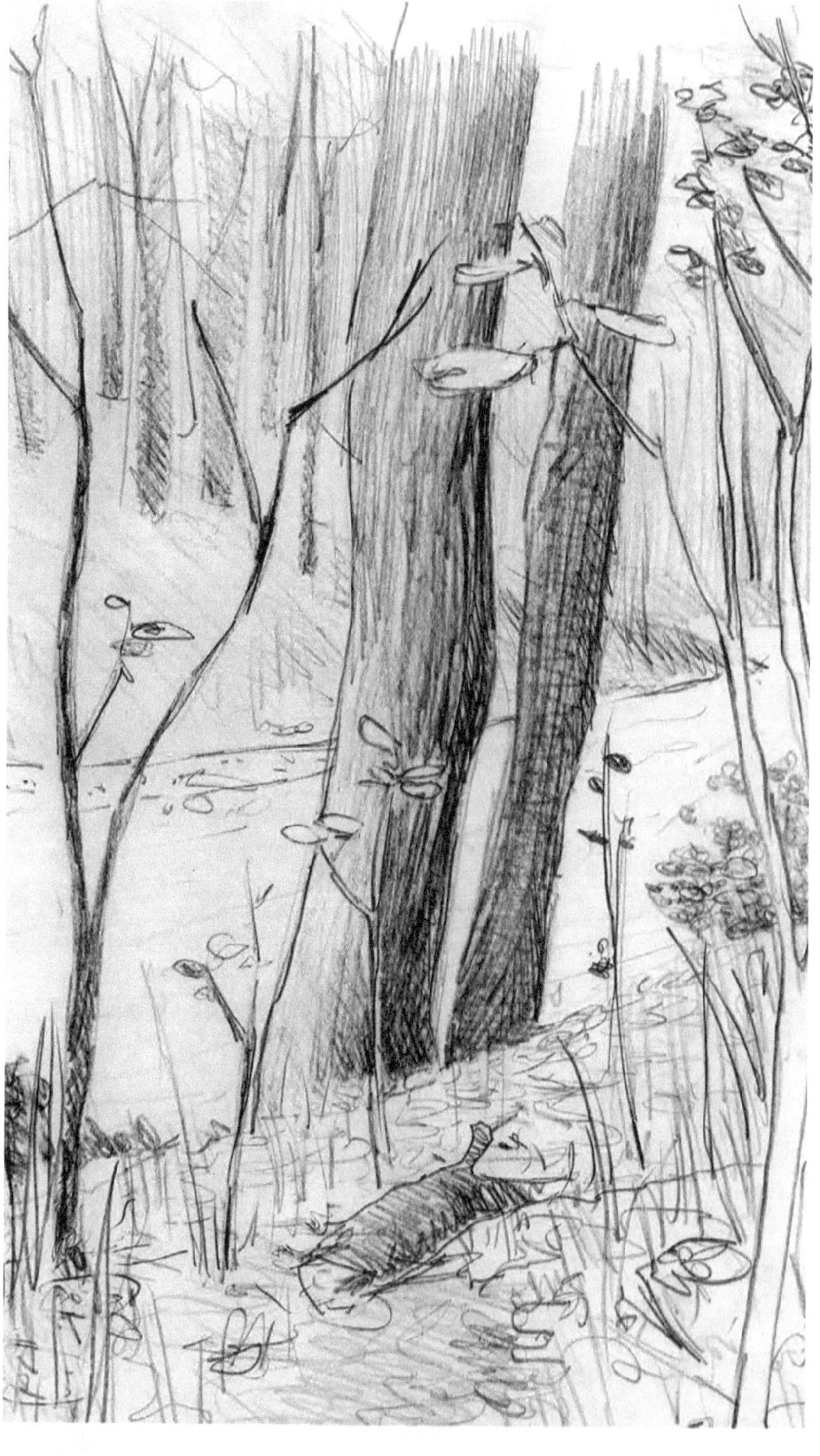

Waypoint Seven

Stream

Now,

I stand on this rich earth—beside Stream.

This morning's walk was rich and full of wonder. It always is, even when I take unintended paths. I hold these encounters precious. Throughout the day…

Yet,

These moments flash in my mind.

When I stand at Stream's side,

My breath stills, my heart calms, my thoughts sleep. I am free from want.

I am a mere speck within all I see and feel and sense.

This anonymous union…

Encloses and comfort me.

The time is now late morning.

Stream traveled a very long way to rest at this juncture. Stream's total journey to this place covered many, many miles—up, down, straight, branching, twisting, bending over different soil and different stone.

At times, Stream was sluggish, stalled, resting, or merely flowing.

At times, flowing with mighty force, but…

Always meandering.

East, from where I sit, I see Stream emerge as a smooth, eighty- degree right bend that travels just a few feet, then swerves left, then flows straight forward past a smaller stream whose water empties into Stream…

Then, onward past where I stand.

I recognize the smaller stream. I watched it begin its journey next to Shadow Pond.

I cannot even guess how many other meandering streams joined with Stream beyond my morning walk.

At this juncture, Stream travels east to west, past where I stand, past the barren field I walked upon when I first began this morning's journey, then far beyond to other places.

From where I stand, I can see Stream about a quarter mile forward west. There, Stream bends even farther west…

Beyond my view.

I linger where my steps halted—to scour my surrounding. Stream's comfort always contrasts with the reality of…

Unexpected danger.

My legs tingle. I feel weary from the morning's walk.

I turn and search for my gutless tree log that I keep hidden between the trees behind me—higher up the descending path.

It is roughly weathered, dark, and softened from laying in the moist earth—so that when I sit, it bends, but does not break. I check inside for unseen varmints that may have nested there.

Finally, just a couple of yards from Stream's edge…

I sit and daydream.

Springtime is almost here, but not quite.

The small buds peeking from the tree limbs say Winter is clearly leaving.

But the foliage looks more like late Autumn.

All around me, I also see various hues of brown and greys, some black, and sparse accents of red or orange or white.

The shallow water along Stream's edges moves quickly and the soon-to-leave-winter-sun bounces sharp rays of light off the moving water.

In the middle of this flow, brown and sometimes green seaweed-like silt covers two-thirds of Stream's water. When I bend to take a handful, the texture feels like slimed grass. It slides through my fingers…

Still it is appealing.

Even though it is likely too early in the season, I bend forward to look for tadpoles or larvae.

I remember when I was a child,

When my friends and I accidently-on-purpose fell into a different stream…

And we were happily dirty and wet.

When we caught mostly tadpoles, but also a few water bugs, flies, diving beetles and rarely, a water scorpion.

When our parents scolded us for shutting the insects inside sealed glass jars.

When we opened the jar caps and some flew, but most did not—even after we put holes in the lids…

And I stopped catching them.

I remember this past Winter Season.
When the air was crisp and clean and free of pollen.

Then, I walked farther east on Stream's icy path, under overarching tree limbs that met in the middle of Stream.

An explosion of sparkles burst outward as fan-shaped rays of sun
fell through the iced branches.

The ensemble of water droplets blurred amidst the sun…
And looked like clouded rain.

Suddenly,

I hear a different sound behind me and turn to look.

As fast as I can blink, I see a hawk swoop toward the earth, clamp
its long talons deep inside a baby bunny, then soar upward and
disappear.

I hear the baby scream. I see the blood fall.

I see the mother run. I feel very tired…
I hide my log, turn, and walk home.

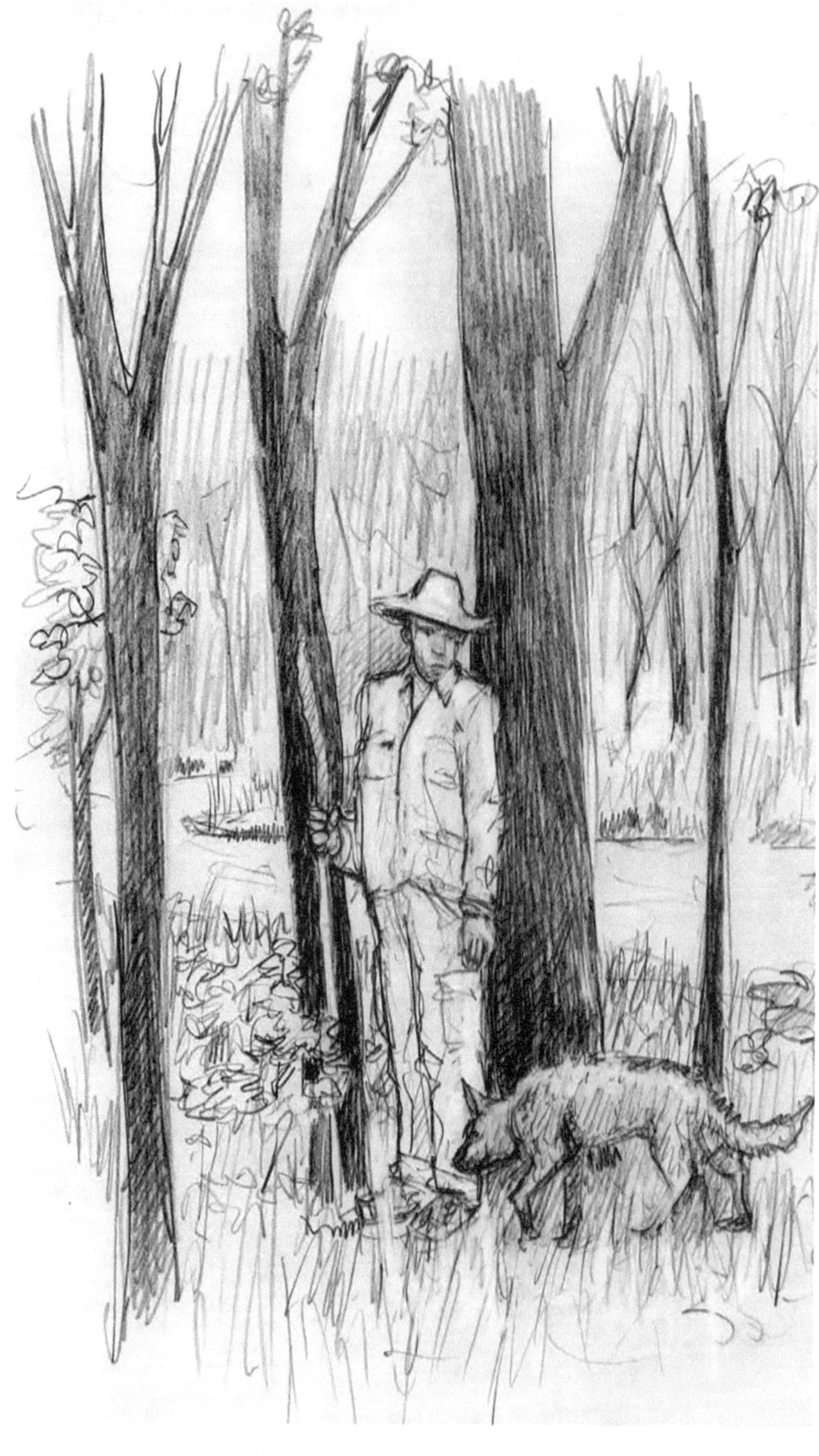

Waypoint Eight

Tree Man

New light shines on this dawn and the air is gently warm. I glance down upon the caged field, and…

All I see is green!

Quickly, I feed the horses, release them to the field, and walk briskly down the hill. As I cross Stream's waters, I note the flow is brisk, but calm.

Three dogs walk with me.
"No," I say, firmly. "Stay!"

All three dogs wag their tails a bit faster and jog onward, quickly reaching the field.

Lucky is a seventy-five-pound, mostly Shepherd cur who came to me from death row. On the night before his scheduled execution, twelve years ago, I said,
"Yes, he can stay, but only…

Until you find him a forever home."

Lucky has the heart of a kitten. Yet he is big with a deep, gravelly bark. Until a person gets to know him, they usually find him scary.

Prince Charming (black and white) and Count Bentley (brown and white) are Shih Tzu's—age ten and seven respectively—each twelve to fifteen pounds. They don't know they are foo-foo dogs. They act like ambitious, dirty, farm dogs…

All three dogs are Macho Males.

Today, I walk directly to Stream. No side excursions.
The dogs and I quickly walk the length of the caged field, go out the black steel gate, turn left, then right, then straight through the wooded path, and across the field of…

The Luckless Deer.

As we near the top of the path that slopes to Stream, something feels different. The dogs are ahead of me, but instead of their

usual habit of going straight down to Stream, they stop. They
travel in circles, sniffing the ground. Then…
> *All three dogs turn and mark that part of the field.*

Lucky veers right, toward the wooded hill that overlooks
Stream. At first, I see nothing unusual. But, as my eyes focus, I
see a non-familiar outline.

Perhaps it is a different shaped tree, a wooden pole, or
sculpted wood?

Gradually, I discern body parts of a slightly plump, pasty-skinned,
white man standing perfectly still and straight, his body touching
a stately, yet wildly branched, tree.

Not even his eyes—fixed behind clear eyeglasses, under a round,
wide-brimmed tan hat—move…
> *He holds a tall walking stick in his right hand.*

I guess he is about five-feet-nine, perhaps sixty years old. He looks
straight at me, silent…
I pause and stare back.

After a bit, I say,
"Hello. I didn't see you there."
No reply.

"Do, you live near here?" I ask.
He nods yes, not moving even one hair. He keeps his eyes on
Lucky who is sniffing his dusty shoes…

Thinking of nothing relevant, like, "What are you doing here?"
I merely ask,
"Do you like dogs?"
I wonder what to think, to do.
He gives no reply, but I see him smirk…
> *It all feels creepy.*

From behind me, I hear noise. I turn and see a familiar, tall, thirty-something, smiling woman, with long brown hair pulled to the back of her head and fastened with a rawhide tie. She rides atop a large brown gelding who walks relaxed, as if he is enjoying a pleasant outing with friends.

In her right hand, the welcome rider holds a separate rein that connects to a well-fleshed, mid-sized brown and white pony.

Atop the pony is a young girl, maybe ten years old, wearing thick eyeglasses that magnify her glaring brown eyes. A black safety helmet covers all but snippets of her blondish hair.

The young girl stares at me—but does not speak, nor smile, nor act as if she heard me say hello. She exhales, grimaces, turns to her leader and utters growling like noises.

In past meetings, she waited too long while her leader and I talked.

Tree Man sees the riders too. "I am a cat person," he says.

Then he turns and walks quickly away in the opposite direction from the horse woman.

Was he harmless?
Maybe.
Was he afraid of Lucky?
Maybe.
Was he Creepy?
Yes!

I walk to Stream, find my hidden log, and sit. I think.

After a bit, I say,

"Stream, I walked this walk to sit by you seven-thousand-two-hundred-eighty-four times. But this is the first day I met a human I thought was unsafe"…

And, this is a very sad fact.

I ask Stream why, but Stream is silent.

I stand and take my log to its safe place.

Maybe tomorrow, Stream will have answers.

As I take a step toward home, I hear a splash behind me.
I turn and see Stream erupt upward, then softly curve, then fall into the Bed below.

The water sparkles, and I hear a pleasant tinkle.

My steps become a soft bounce toward home.
The dogs run to join me, tails wagging.

A Note:
Five days per week times fifty-two weeks equals two hundred and sixty days times twenty-eight years equals seven thousand, two hundred, and eighty days of fearless walks with Nature.

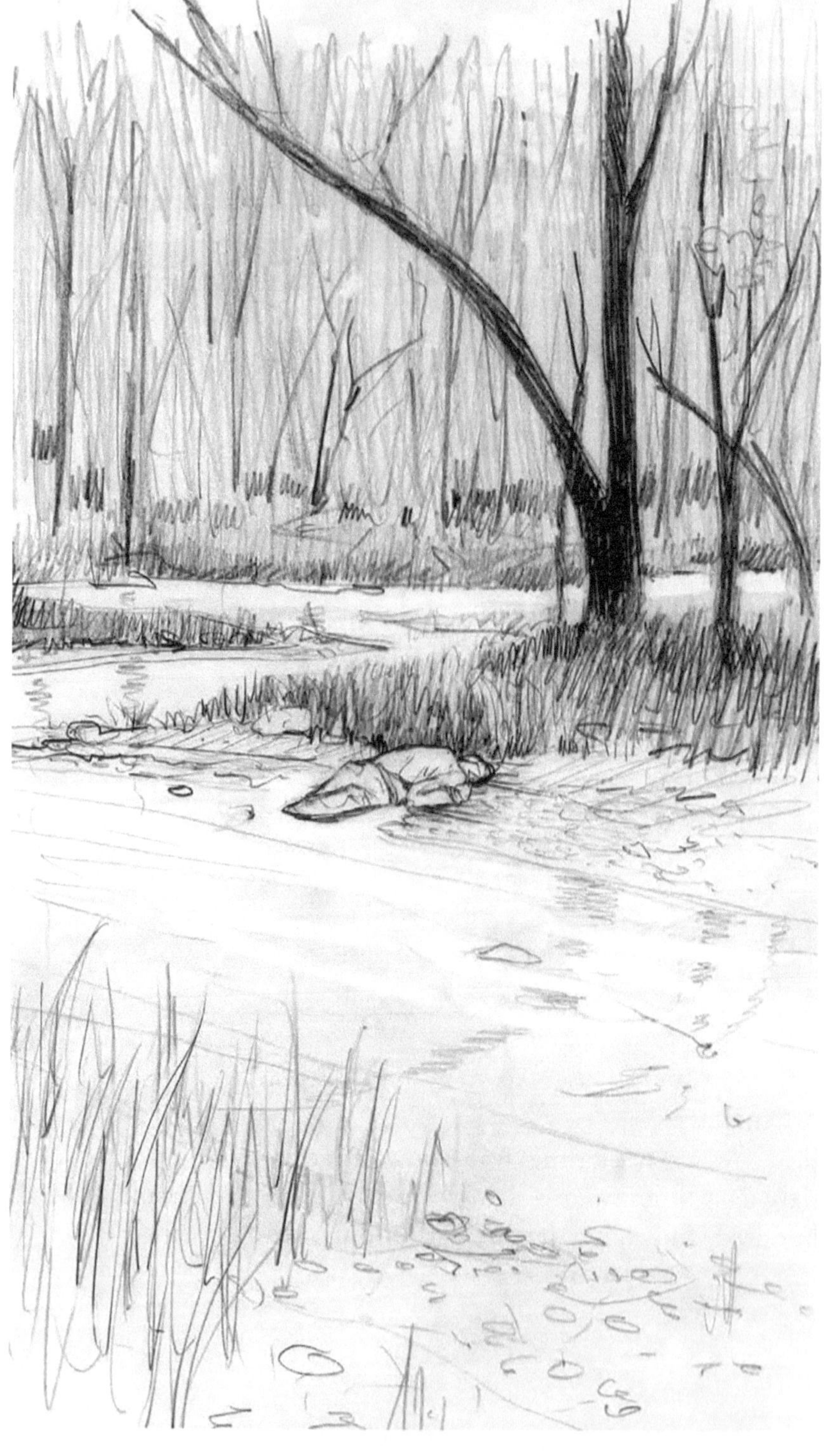

Waypoint Nine

Stream's Reply

Next day, sometime near noon, at home, As I watch TV, resting, subdued, weary.

A news flash appears on the local station, Words of the news reporter intrude…

An unidentified, slightly overweight white man, judged to be about sixty, was found dead this afternoon, near a local stream. Apparently, the man was walking in or near the stream and was caught in unexpected flooding water.

If you have related information, please call the local police.

Wow! I feel chills.

I arise and go to Stream—at my usual place. I need to check, to be sure.

But, once there, I cannot find my log. Anywhere!

I slowly begin the journey home. My feet feel heavy. My shoulders slump. I have no will to straighten.

I walk slowly forward, then pause to breathe deeply.

I accept.

But then…
Just a few steps farther…
I see it!
I see my log! My log is safe!
Yes. Yes. Yes!
Thank you Stream

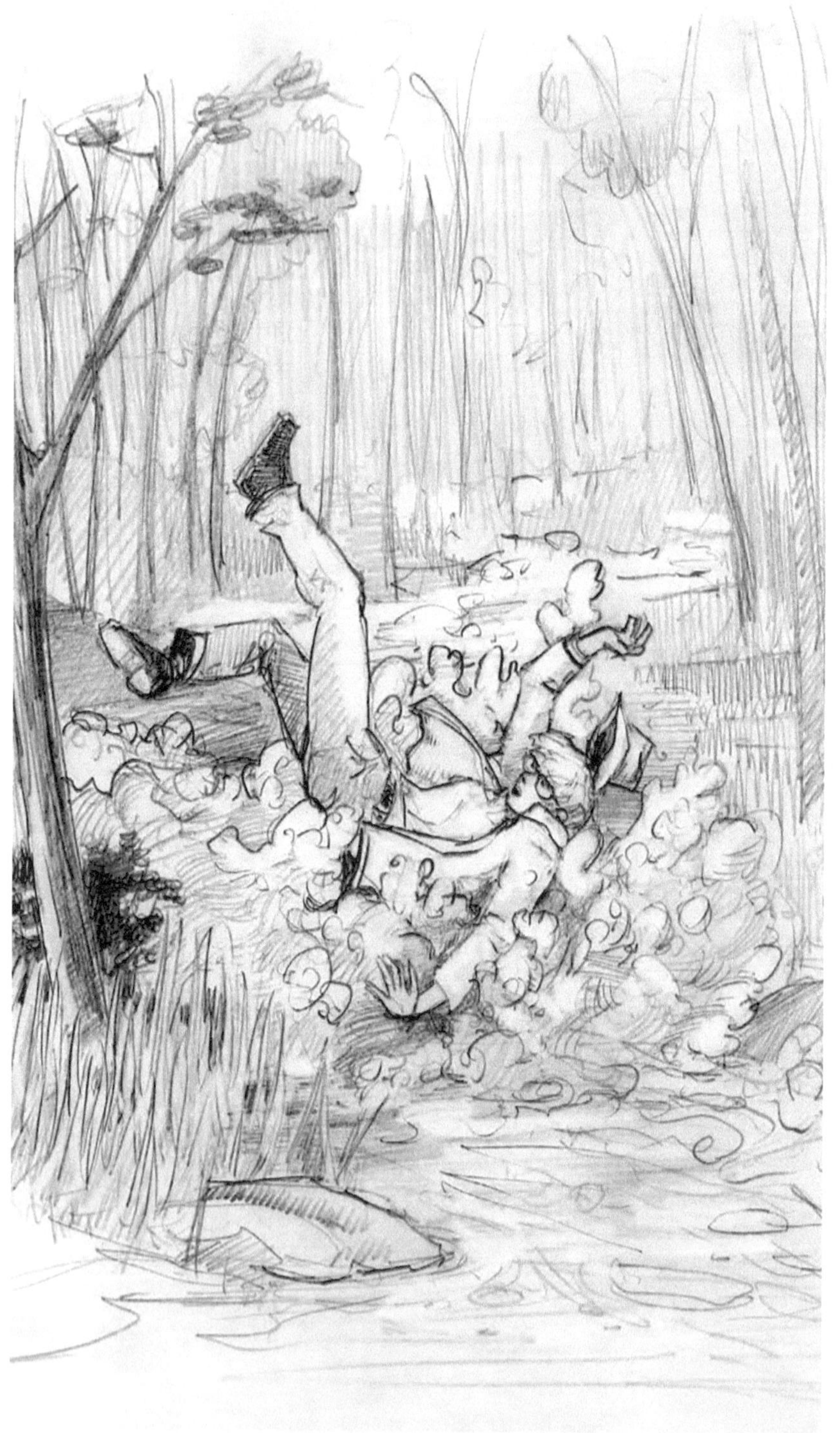

Waypoint Ten

Stream Ride

I am no one in particular. I am everyone who is conscious of their unity with nature.

On another morning, I was walking in the woods and came upon Stream at a different site than the one I usually visit.

Stream was wandering lazily along a winding rock bed.

"Are you having an interesting trip?" I asked.
"Very interesting," Stream said. "Every turn brings mystery."
"May I ride along with you?" I asked.
"Of course," Stream said. "I gather lots of interesting chaps as I travel. And you look dapper."

I was dumbstruck, enthralled. Stream was inviting *Me*.

Exciting!

"Don't get behind," Stream said. "Come on! Let's mosey along together."

"You bet," I said as I put one foot and then the other into Stream's travel road, the Bed.

"I'm in. You are not going without me."

"Ha, ha. That might be a dangerous decision," Stream said. "Stay attentive. Maybe it will be dull and maybe it won't."

Stream tinkled while flowing a bit more rapidly over the rocks.

The walk was relaxing, and the view was amazing. On the banks, wildflowers erratically appeared as though they chose to blossom just for me... and for Stream.

Trillium, wild strawberries wandering up and down the banks, button shrubs, crested blue iris and wild cilantro stared back at every turn. Purple cone flowers, just greening, peeked through the dark lush soil.

I breathed the beauty and thanked Stream for inviting me.

But I was so relaxed I failed to sense the danger that lay behind.

At the next turn, I suddenly became aware of dark clouds and my view shadowed. My feet felt the rush of water so I stepped more quickly, not so much at will, but like being pushed along.

"Why was there a roar?"

My answer came quickly. From the meandering streams!

Mounds of hostile, brush-filled, fallen rain violently rushed down the hills behind and aimed straight for Stream…and me!

My unwilling limbs took turns bouncing above and rolling under the rushing water as it slammed powerfully—mastering everything it touched.

The harsh water had hit Stream—violently.

Then, I felt my body fly in the air.

Before I felt nothing, I saw my feet above my body.

As my eyes saw once again, I found myself lying in a still wet field, empty of traveling waves… and knew I was lucky.

Stream was lost, unseen, beneath the hostile water that invaded our tranquil friendship.

I walked away in numbness, not knowing how my friend had fared, unable to help.

A few days later, when my yielding body was less sore, I returned to check on Stream.

I noticed that Stream's bed was deeper, but not yet carved so violently as to lose the self that I knew.

That would come later.
"How are you Stream?" I asked.

"I am quite well, thank you. This was not a new journey for me. It is a part of who I am—a journey I will experience again."

"But, how are You?"

"I am also well, my friend. Sore, but well," I replied, and continued.

"It was indeed an adventurous walk with you, Stream."

"It awakened primitive urges sparked by unstoppable life passions I won't forget."

"I will store our journey carefully amidst primal genes that carry messages to future generations."

"When we are both unseen, our experience will still live."

Then, finally, I whispered, "Our day was special, Stream."

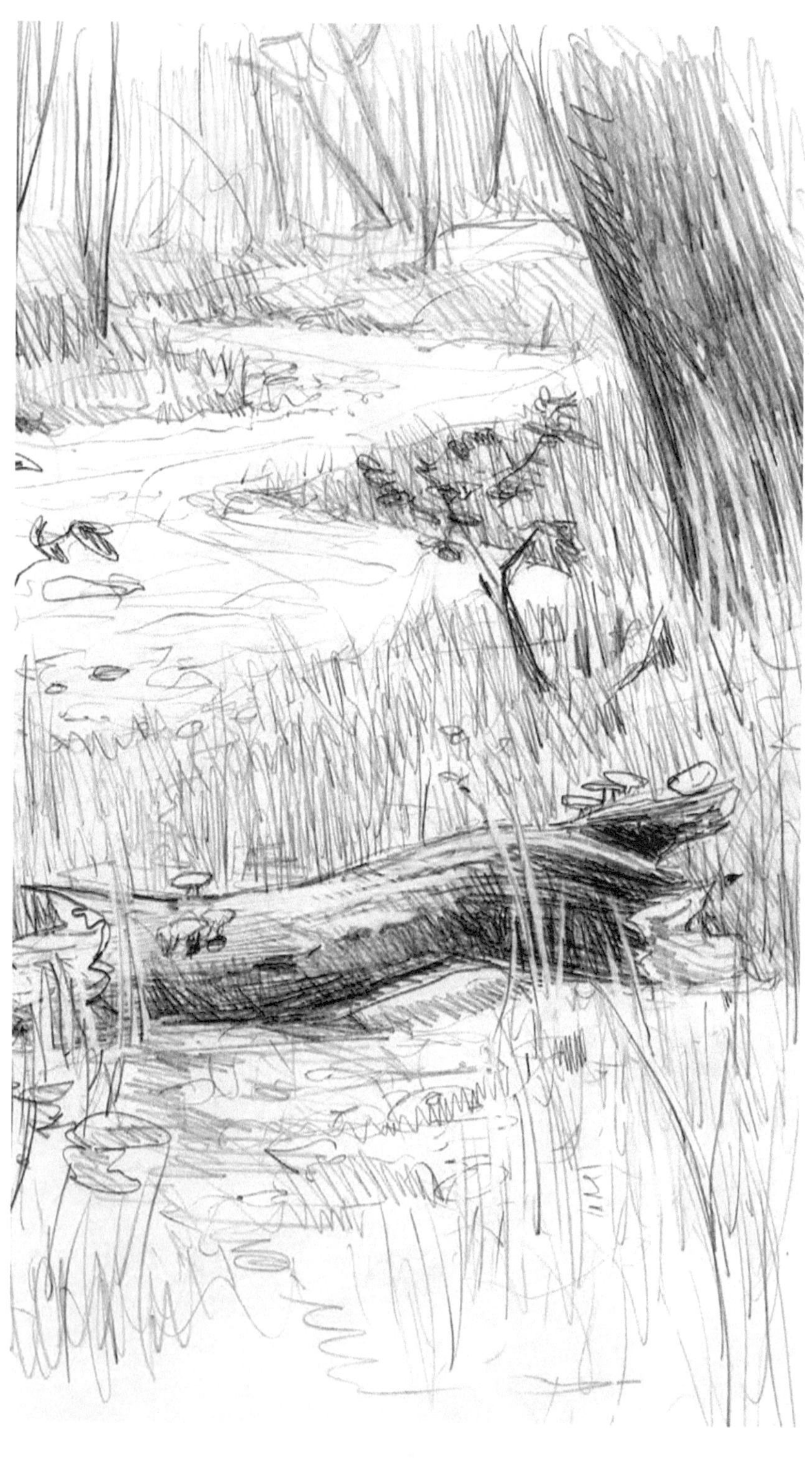

Waypoint Eleven

WHEN

Let me be a dreamer in love with a running, singing, bubbling, happy stream who yet stands ready to birth harsh angry waves.

Let me call Stream to warm my restless soul, calm my mind, and quench this unquieted thirst of my sleeping ancient genes that nudge me relentlessly to connect.

Let me fling away laughter that names me strange.

Let me go even deeper in union with this unexpected lover. It is with Stream that I know the spirit of times past.

It is with Stream that youth joins age and differences dissolve.

It is my heritage that guides me. Stream sees me standing tall and joins me with remembrance of past figures as they rose from four to two.

Let me stay my love for all the days I live, and

When I die, let me slowly dissolve and become unseen, yet still there, a part of all Streams past and yet to be.

And that my friend, is the end of a Stream of a Story.

About the Author

Who am I? A wannabe writer since age thirteen when I announced to my uppity city cousin, "I am going to write and publish a book when I am grown!" I did not know how or when I would complete my teen vision. Black Beauty was my favorite book. I loved horses. Still do. My book might have been a horse and girl adventure. When I grew to a woman, I did write. A lot! I wrote a doctoral dissertation, Maybe that was the book? No! I became a practicing nurse and nurse educator. I published about fifty peer-reviewed health research articles and secured several successful grant awards. Nope! I still was not the writer I wanted to be. I retired. I wrote about childhood memories while living on a Union County farm—a corn field, a chicken house, riding away from home at midnight on my black quarter horse, returning before my parents awakened. Two a.m. on a dark, empty country road gave me pause. Where was I going? Where will I stay? I had no money. The worst of this adventure was that no one, except my horse, knew I ran away. I did write a story, but not a book, about this adventure. I enrolled at Spalding University in their awesome creative writing program. I wrote profiles of interesting older women who lived in an underserved neighborhood in Louisville, Kentucky. I am near finishing and publishing these. But, one day I paused to listen to my soul. I picked up a pen and wrote *Stream*. This book is an ode to the rhythm of nature. I believe *Stream* speaks to our soul and invites the reader to consider their spiritual connection to nature. I believe *Stream* nourishes the core of who we are as humans living on this good earth. I hope this book inspires the reader to seek, or continue to seek, sustenance from nature. And to do their part to protect nature for those who shall come after us. I invite you to read *Stream*!

Kay Long Roberts